# Do As I Say, Not As I Do

Reflections, Life Lessons & Advice for Daughters

# Do As I Say, Not As I Do

Reflections, Life Lessons & Advice for Daughters

## DR. TAMMY JAMESON

*For my daughter, Sejal.*
*We argue, fight, dance, and laugh. You get on my nerves*
*at times, but I wouldn't change one thing about you.*
*I love you and I'm very proud of you. Thanks for saving*
*my life and being my inspiration.*

**DO AS I SAY, NOT AS I DO**
Published by Purposely Created Publishing Group™

Copyright © 2016 Tammy Jameson
ALL RIGHTS RESERVED.

Printed in the United States of America

ISBN (ebook): 978-1-942838-93-7

ISBN (paperback): 978-1-942838-92-0

Special discounts are available on bulk quantity purchases by book clubs, associations, and special interest groups. For details email: sales@publishyourgift.com or call (888) 949-6228.

*For information logon to:*
www.PublishYourGift.com

# Table of Contents

# Introduction

*My road to becoming a mother:*

I was a senior in college when I found out that I was pregnant. At first, my friends and I thought that I had a virus, so I was given all kinds of low-country concoctions to help me get over my "virus." Of course, none of them helped. I remember, one day, being bent over a toilet in my friend's off-campus trailer, feeling as if I would just die. My friend, who thought she was an expert in detecting pregnancy symptoms, burst through the door to see if my vomit looked like orange juice. She carefully peered into the toilet and yelled "Oh my god! Girl, you're pregnant!" I thought to myself, "You have got to be kidding me!" There was no way that I could be pregnant! I had always been careful—I was in a committed relationship, but still I used protection. No way! I needed proof.

Within minutes we were flying down Highway 301 in Mitzi (what we called my friend's little gray Mazda), headed towards one of those free health clinics. The place stunk of ass and cleaning solution, the floors looked like they hadn't been cleaned in years, and the walls had dirt and scuff marks on them. I didn't want to touch anything in there and I didn't want anything in there touching me. The clinic was disgusting which made me even more ashamed and embarrassed to be there. Had I stooped this low?

After waiting for about an hour, I was finally called to the back where I was grilled harder than someone on trial for murder. I was given a cup to piss in and sent to a bathroom that was even more disgusting than the waiting area. I waited for what seemed like years for the results. Then, a nurse appeared and exclaimed, "You're the lucky winner!"

I looked around to see who she was talking to, because surely she wasn't talking to me! I know that she wasn't putting all of my business out there like that! Of course, she was. I slumped down in my chair in disbelief and tried to process what I was just told.

If I was the lucky winner, why did I feel as if I had lost everything? I was pregnant, knocked up, with child—a baby mama. The thought of being anyone's baby mama made me sick to my stomach. I cried and cried and cried, thinking that my life was over. I had dreams: I had plans to move to New York after graduation to become a writer. I wasn't planning on being anybody's mama. Even more than my own disappointment, I was overcome with sadness when I thought about upsetting my parents and everyone else who had believed in me.

I called home to tell my parents the news. My dad was upset; he didn't say much. I was hysterical and crying, but, to my surprise, my mother was calm. I thought that she would disown me or throw the pregnancy up in my face, since I had always disappointed her in one way or another. But she told me that this was not the end of the world and that I was going to be okay. When she didn't react the way that I thought she would, I was relieved and, for the first time, I believed that I would be okay. The last thing that I needed was to fall out with my mother when I needed her most—her encouragement and support were priceless. I didn't know if I could handle the responsibility, but having an abortion was not an option for me. I had to take responsibility for my actions and do the right thing. I had reassurance that, by keeping the baby, I was making the right decision.

### A snapshot into my life as a mother:

I had no idea if the baby was a boy or a girl. I wanted to be surprised. Five weeks before my college graduation and four days after Biggie was killed, I was induced into labor. This baby was overdue and did not want to come—I should've known that I was in trouble!

My mother was right there like she said she would be, like she always had been. It was all the support that I needed. I refused any medication and had a natural birth, so I remember being in a lot of pain until I heard my mother ask, "What we got, Doc?"

The doctor happily exclaimed that I had given birth to a girl. At the time, I was just glad that it was over. I named her Sejal, which means "to bring love and new beginnings into life." My mother couldn't wait to put my daughter in my arms, but

I was tired. I wanted to hold her, just not at that very moment. Didn't she know what I had just gone through?

"I'll hold her later," I told my mother. "I have forever."

I was determined to graduate on time so, two weeks after giving birth, I returned to South Carolina State University to complete my undergraduate degree. I didn't have a babysitter, so my instructors agreed to let me bring Sejal to class with me if I sat in the back and she was quiet. So, I took her to every class in her carrier and sat in the back of the room. No one ever knew she was there unless they saw her.

In honesty, I was embarrassed and ashamed that I was even in that situation. I had become exactly what I never wanted to be: a statistic. A few of my professors didn't let me forget it either. I was ridiculed. One even advised me to quit college, but that was not an option for me. I was a lot of things, but a quitter was not one of them.

It was a struggle, but we made it through those tough times. My daughter was five-weeks old when I graduated from college, which happened to be on Mother's Day. It was the happiest day of my life! We had done it! Right then, I knew she and I would be okay and that we were destined for great things. We had each other. I knew that then that even when she grew up, no matter what, she would always be my Sejal.

### My daughter was taking notice

Sejal was always an outspoken child. Not disrespectful, but inquisitive. I tried to teach her everything that I knew about being a strong, independent woman, all while being in an abusive relationship. Who was I fooling? I wasn't the woman I was trying to teach her to be and she saw right through me.

Once, when she was five, we were riding in the car. I had picked her up from school and was headed home. I was sad, which was usual at that time of my life. My life was in shambles and I had no idea how to fix it. I was silent. On the other hand, Sejal was a chatterbox: I would ask her how her day went and she could go on, and on, and on. I didn't mind; I wanted her to always feel that she could talk to me. And that day she did. She told me exactly what she was thinking, and I was not prepared.

She said, "Mommy, I never want to be like you when I grow up."

Of course I was completely thrown off and asked her why. She then went on to say that she would never let anyone, especially a man, disrespect her and treat her bad the way that I did in my abusive marriage. She then became quiet, waiting for my response. Only, I didn't have one. I usually had a response for her questions and comments, but I had nothing! I was tapped out of explanations, because she was absolutely right.

I don't know what hurt me more: the fact that I had gotten checked by a five-year-old or the fact that my daughter said she never wanted to be the woman I was. But how could I blame her? *I* didn't want to be the woman I was at that point in my life. I was unhappy, abused, and unappreciated. A doormat.

It took me a few years after that conversation to free myself of the negativity and abuse that I suffered, but I rebuilt myself brick by brick until I was a wall that could not be torn down by anyone else's words or actions. I learned to love myself and life again. I was a strong woman, my own person. I loved Sejal for teaching me that I had to be a better example of a woman.

### Borrowed time

It wasn't until Sejal was a senior in high school that I realized that my time with her was limited. Wait! I needed more time! I had so many things that I felt I didn't get to teach her. She needed more time! Like most eighteen-year-olds, she felt like she had everything all figured out, like someone flipped a switch and she was suddenly grown! She didn't want to listen to anything that I had to say, and she thought she could talk to me in any kind of way. I didn't know who this girl thought she was, but it certainly wasn't the young woman that I had raised.

A very good friend gave me some great advice. She told me that my job as a mother is never over, but at eighteen, my daughter needed less of a mother and more of a mentor to guide her through womanhood. She needed a friend to help her through the next chapters of her life. She was too old for me to teach her anything else. Of course, she had to figure out some things on her own, but I could help her through the growing pains and be there for her without being an authoritative, overwhelming presence. I could let her be who she is, yet still advise her.

Almost immediately, I felt the need to jot down every great idea or word of advice that I had ever heard over the years or was given to me from my own mother. Things that I thought she should know and needed to know as a woman. Things that I did not know at her age, but wish I had. It gave me the chills just thinking about who or what I could have been had I known all of life's little secrets. So, while I was thinking of the greatest coming of age gift that I could give my daughter, I thought, "Why not give her the gift of knowledge?" The gift of knowing now what she would come to know when she was much older.

Moms have tons of advice for their daughters. When they are younger, it might be "Cross your legs at the ankle when you wear a dress," "Stand up straight," or "Don't sit on anyone's lap." Some of these words of wisdom are soon forgotten, but other advice lasts a lifetime. I've asked some of my friends and family members to share the most important advice they've given their daughters. I've shared some of my own advice to my daughter as well.

Here are words of advice worth remembering.

# Chapter 1:
# Lawd Have Mercy!

Most people have some belief that there is a higher being. No matter what we call him, there is someone greater than ourselves who we pray to and seek guidance from. Spirituality keeps us grounded and gives us a moral code to live by.

When my daughter was five, she started praying for a "baby brother." I kept telling her that it wasn't going to happen, but night after night when she said her prayers, she asked God to bless everyone from me all the way to the dog down the street. Her prayers always ended with "And God *please* give me a baby brother!"

I would sit on the edge of her bed trying to hold back tears of laughter, because I knew that I certainly was not having another child. This went on for about a year, until one day, she began ending her prayers with "God, thank you for my baby brother." I had no idea what she was talking about; I had no intentions of having another child. When she flat out told me that I was pregnant, I laughed at her and said, "Oh, yeah, I'd like to see that!"

Well, lo and behold, a couple of weeks later I missed my period. I went to the doctor and was told that I was pregnant. I couldn't believe it. When I told my daughter the news, she wasn't surprised at all. She didn't even look up as she combed her dolls hair.

All she said was "I told you!"

Four months later I found out that the gender of the baby was a boy. I used to wonder if Sejal was psychic. How did she know that I was having a son? But today, I think of how my daughter spoke my son into existence. She had faith and believed that her prayers would be answered. There is definitely power in prayer.

In regards to spirituality:

**1. Always put God first in all that you do.** Do this and everything will fall into place. Always.

**2. Make sure that you have a personal relationship with God.** A relationship that's all your own in which you can talk to Him about any and everything, knowing that He is there listening, waiting for you to cast your cares upon Him.

**3. It would be great if you go to a worship service from time to time.** But always know that church is in your heart, not in a physical building. Don't beat yourself up if you don't bust through the doors of a church every Sunday.

**4. Tithing does not always mean giving 10% of your income.** You can tithe by dedicating your time, efforts, and talents to helping others.

**5. What you put out in the universe is what you will get.** If you put our negative thoughts, you will be negative. If you want a positive life and positive outcomes, think positive!

**6. There's nothing "religious" about threats.** Sometimes, people send silly chain emails that demand you forward the message or "God will curse you." Remember that God is not vindictive and doesn't operate in that way.

**7. Have faith, even when there seems to be no solution in sight.** A little faith will open doors that you never imagined and take you to places that you've never seen.

**8. Don't believe the hype.** Everyone that goes to church is not a Christian and does not always follow Christian principles. Do not look to people for guidance—always look to God. People will disappoint you, but God won't.

**9. Be careful of what you pray for.** You just might get it… and not like it!

**10. Trust in the Lord with all of your heart and lean not on your own understanding.** Don't expect your parents to know all of the answers. They don't have them.

**11. If God has blessed you with a gift, use it.** God gives us all gifts. Find your gift, and use it or lose it!

**12. There is power in prayer.** Prayer does work. Sometimes, we pray for things and expect God to simply give, but it doesn't always work that way. You won't always receive answers when you want them, but when He answers them, it will be what you need when you need it.

# Chapter 2:
## It's All About You

You've probably heard your mother or someone close to you tell you once or even twice that it's not all about you. Well, I agree and disagree with this statement. We live in a selfish society, where everything is I, I, I or me, me, me. It's easy for us to focus solely on what we want and need. After all, life is what *we* make it right?

Here's the thing: it *is* all about you. But before you start doing cartwheels, I want you to truly think about what that statement means. Yes, it is all about you—it's about your actions, thoughts, words, and attitude. That means that you have to be cognizant of what you say and do. Nine times out of ten, it's your actions and words that prevent you from being in a position to receive. Making life all about you does not give you a pass to be a selfish bitch. What it does is hold *you* accountable for what *you* put in the universe. When you focus only on yourself, you miss the big picture of what life is truly about.

Life is about using your gifts and talents to make a positive contribution to society. It's not about manipulating people and situations so that things work in your favor. Once you get over yourself, you'll be in more of a position to receive all that life has to offer.

**1. You are beautiful, talented, and highly favored.** Don't compare yourself to others. There's only one YOU. You are special.

**2. Attitude is everything.** If you have the right attitude, you can overcome anything.

**3. Always be a lady.** I don't care how bad you want to curse someone out or how ratchet you want to be. Always carry yourself like a woman of class. You'll be respected more if you do.

**4. Never make excuses.** If you don't want to appear incompetent, don't make excuses. Excuses are useless. No one respects someone who always has an excuse for not doing what they were supposed to do or said they would do. If for some reason you aren't able to do what was expected of you, just admit that you dropped the ball. Own your shit!

**5. Always know when you should shut up and color.** All battles are not yours to fight. Learn how to pick your battles. Sometimes it's best to keep your mouth closed, especially when you don't know what you're talking about.

**6. Listen more than you open your mouth.** You can't hear if you are always running your mouth.

7. There is a time and place for everything. There will never be a right time for showing your ass in the street. However, it's perfectly fine to show your ass in the comfort of your own home where no one can see you making a fool out of yourself.

**8. Life is what *you* make of it.** You are in control of your happiness. If you don't like the direction your life is going in, change routes. In the end, you cannot blame anyone else for your unhappiness.

**9. Always find time for selfless acts of kindness.** Do something nice for others without expecting anything in return. Putting a smile on someone else's face is good for the soul. Let your words and actions come from your heart; otherwise, keep your half-assed efforts to yourself.

**10. Ratchet is not the new classy and it never will be.** There is nothing cute about being ratchet or a "bad bitch," period. The way you carry yourself is how you will be treated. Would you rather be treated like a classy woman or a ratchet, bad bitch? Trust me, there's a difference. Strive to be a respected woman. Think about how you would like to be perceived at fifty—you make the choice!

**11. No one walking this earth owes you anything.** If you want something, work hard to earn it yourself. Be appreciative when someone does something for you.

**12. In this world, there are givers and takers.** Givers unselfishly give to others expecting nothing in return, while takers feel entitled and will suck you dry. Takers are users. Never be a user, because if you do, you will suck!

**13. Have compassion.** You never know what someone else is going through. They may be having the worst day of their life. Try to keep that in mind the next time you are about to go off on someone.

**14. Don't let anger be a feeling that makes your mouth work faster than your thoughts.** Be slow to speak when you're angry. Once words leave your mouth, you cannot take them back no matter how much you apologize.

**15. Learn not to take everything personally.** Every situation is not all about you. Having thick skin will protect you and your feelings.

**16. Sometimes it's better to keep your mouth shut and let people think you are an idiot than to open your mouth and remove all doubt.** If you don't know what you're talking about, shut up! Making assumptions will only make you look like the dumbass.

**17. Nothing will change for you until the pain of staying the same is greater than the pain of change.** Things won't change for you until you are tired of being tired.

**18. Nothing is open past two am except whores and 7-11.** If a man only wants to see you late at night, he is degrading your self-respect. Don't be a booty call.

**19. Make a "things-to-do" list daily.** It'll help you manage your time and remind you of what you need to do.

**20. Always enjoy the simple things in life.** It's the little things that matters most.

**21. Be on time.** When you are on someone else's time, be on time and do not have them waiting on you.

**22. What you say with your face says it all.** You can say one thing, but if your facial expressions say another, it will be a dead giveaway that you are lying.

**23. Always make time to do the things you love.** If you don't have a hobby, get one! You will get more enjoyment out of life.

**24. Your business is your business.** Everything is not meant to be shared. Keep some things to yourself.

**25. One day you'll just be a memory to someone.** Do your best to be a good one.

**26. Keep your priorities in order.** Always remember what is important; it will keep you grounded.

**27. There will always be someone smarter, prettier, and thinner than you.** But there is only one you. Be comfortable with who you are.

**28. If you can't be positive, keep your mouth shut.** Nothing is worse than someone with negative energy.

**29. There is no yellow brick road to happiness.** If you don't like the path you're on, change roads. You lead your life; it doesn't lead you.

**30. Life is not a fairytale.** Losing your shoe at midnight doesn't mean that you're Cinderella. It means that you had one too many.

**31. Don't let others determine your worth.** You determine your worth—it comes from inside and it's who you are. Others' opinions don't make you who you are. Be proud of the abilities and talents that make you special.

**32. You were born to shine.** Live life with boldness and passion knowing that you are destined for greatness. You're a superstar!

**33. Help others in need.** Always be willing to help others, because when the focus is off of yourself, you don't have time to become a selfish or self-absorbed.

**34. It's okay to say "No."** Sure, you don't like it when someone *refuses you or your requests*, but, in life, you will be faced with hard choices. It's perfectly fine to say "No," or sometimes when required, "Hell no!" You have a little voice inside that tells you something doesn't feel right. Listen to your inner voice and respect it. Don't do things that you don't want to do simply out of fear of saying "No." It won't be easy but you'll be glad you did.

**35. Life is unpredictable.** There will be twists and turns in life, but it's how you deal with adversity that makes you successful.

**36. It's not all about you.** Seriously, it isn't!

# Chapter 3:
# Goal Digger

My daughter's first semester of college was challenging. She was adjusting and trying to figure out where she belonged. All her life she dreamed of being a pediatrician and now, through her hard work and dedication, she was pursuing her dreams. I'm sure that she felt a tremendous amount of pressure and wondered how she would measure up against the other pre-med students. Sejal has always been strong, so I knew that she would not become a follower—that was the last thing that I had to worry about when it came to her. I just prayed that she wasn't the half-assed student that I had been in college. The thought of her following in my footsteps made me want to throw up.

Because I didn't want her to fail, I micromanaged everything that had to do with her and college. I knew all the passwords to her school portals and e-mail, which I added to my smart phone so that I could track what was going on. I was an overbearing bitch! I did way too much, thinking that I was helping her, but instead I was only crippling her. After a couple of months of being all up in her business, I was the one who became mentally drained. I was exhausted and angry—I *had* to let her go. I had to trust that the young lady that I raised was more than capable of achieving her goals without my involvement.

I prayed for the strength to let go and gave her to God. Then, one day, without warning it happened! I stopped worrying. I let go and let God. It sounds so cliché, but it worked. I realized that my daughter has always been a goal digger, and although she was faced with some challenges, I knew that she would be all right in the end. She was in God's hands, which was so much better than being in mine.

**1. Set goals and stick to them.** Always have goals and never be complacent. Set goals to achieve them.

**2. Timing is everything.** There's a fine line between persistence and desperation!

**3. The purpose of setting goals isn't to win first place.** The purpose of setting goals is to grow.

**4. Don't set low goals that you know you can reach out of fear of failure.** So, you didn't meet your big goals—look at the work you put in to getting where you are now. You've grown to become more than you were when you started.

**5. Set goals that challenge you.** You'll never achieve greatness if you're complacent.

**6. Prioritize your goals.** List your goals and prioritize them by using a time projection for each. Write the time that you seriously would like to have that particular goal accomplished by, so that you may get an idea of what needs to be started right now and what can wait.

**7. Don't let fear drive you.** Don't let fear of the unknown stop you from achieving greatness!

**8. Life is about growth.** If you are in the same place in life at twenty-five as you were at eighteen, you need to reevaluate how you are doing things. You should not be the same person that you were last year.

**9. Define your own greatness.** Don't let other people convince you that you should adopt their ideas of greatness. Figure out what makes you happy and what makes you feel like a conqueror—let that be your motivation.

**10. Self-motivate.** Don't wait for someone else to motivate you, because you may wait forever. If you want to do something, do it! Don't wait for someone else's time or approval.

**11. Do things on your terms.** You are in charge of your destiny. If you think something is unproductive or isn't the right fit for you, don't do it. What someone else thinks you need may not be what you want.

**12. Invest in yourself.** Figure out what will take you to the next level. It may cost time and money, but it's important to build your brand. Grind and shine.

**13. Be your own she-ro.** Never depend on someone else to save you. If you wait on someone else, you may never get the help you need.

**14. No one can stop you from doing anything but *you*.** If there's something that you want to do in life, just do it. Sounds cliché, but it's that simple. No one can stop you from achieving your goals unless you allow them to.

**15. Get out of your own way.** Don't let self-doubt stop you from doing anything. Sometimes we sabotage our own plan by not believing in ourselves. Don't be afraid to take chances. Sometimes you will fail, but that's okay. Learn from it and keep moving!

# Chapter 4:
# Never Work a Day in Your Life

L et's be real; if you had the choice between staying in bed and going to work, which would you prefer? If I'm guessing correctly, you would stay in bed. I've been working since I was fourteen. I've had shitty jobs and I've had jobs that I've loved. In my twenties, there was a period where I would get unhappy with a job and quit. To this day, I don't remember all of the reasons why I dropped those jobs, but I can assure you that it had less to do with the job and more to do with me. I had always been a wild child, never liking to be told what to do. I would go from job to job doing whatever I wanted, then get mad when someone said anything to me. I was a hothead and no one could tell me anything. As a result, I burned a lot of bridges.

As I became older, I changed my way of thinking. I stopped thinking about what others were doing to me and started thinking of what I was doing to myself. I evaluated my actions and began to realize the role that I played in certain incidences—if I had been a manager at any of my jobs, I would've fired me immediately.

Today, I enjoy getting up and going to work. Why? Because I love what I do. I am paid to perform certain duties, I perform those duties to the best of my abilities, and I go home. I realize that if I'm asked to do something, there's a reason. More importantly, I don't take anything personally. It's just business and that's something that you should always understand. You may not like what you are doing, but if you are getting paid to perform a task, then you should take your ass into work and do what you are required to do. Remember: it's not personal, it's business. Once you get that, you'll never work a day in your life again.

**1. Set yourself up for success.** Choose situations that challenge, teach, and align you with amazing people. You will be rewarded over time.

**2. Always be on time**. If you're going to be late, call and let someone know, so that they know you acknowledge your tardiness and that you respect other people's time.

**3. Be positive.** No one likes working with a Negative Nancy. Bring a positive, can-do attitude with you to work.

**4. Learn new things.** Take on new challenges, and don't be afraid of stepping out of your comfort zone and learning something new.

**5. Work first, play later.** It's simple: take care of your business first, then have a good time.

**6. Bootlickers aren't respected.** Just do your job and you'll be respected more.

**7. Do your best, always.** If someone is paying you to do a job, do your best. If you clean windows, be the best window cleaner in the business. Take pride in everything that you do.

**8. Don't have your name associated with bullshit.** That goes for everything from office gossip to work tasks that you are responsible for. You shouldn't want anyone to think anything less than the best of you.

**9. Know your assets.** Your unique package of skills and expertise, refined through education, experiences, sweat, and tears, is the most valuable asset you'll ever own.

**10. Educate yourself.** Keep your learning power strong by signing up for training sessions, workshops, and college courses that expand your capabilities and make you more marketable. Most employers offer tuition reimbursement opportunities! Take advantage of them to minimize your out-of-pocket expenses.

**11. Learn to swim so you won't drown.** There are going to be plenty of times when you feel stuck in life and your career and become unsure of what to do next (I've been there), don't drown in self-pity and feel overwhelmed. The best way to move forward is to challenge yourself and see what you're made of. Explore new opportunities, even if you don't know where they might take you.

**12. Be bold**. Have the courage to speak up for yourself. Ask for professional favors. Seek help if you need it. Being shy gets you nowhere and only alienates you.

**13. Leave work at work.** Do not take issues or stress from work home with you. Learn how to disconnect. As important as it is for you to work hard, it's just as important for you to have a social life. Give yourself a chance to recharge on a daily basis. Cut off your phone. Turn off the TV. Shut down the computer and go outside. Read. Listen to music. Dance. Be creative. I don't care what you're doing as long as it isn't work-related. Work should not be your entire life.

**14. Get comfortable with being uncomfortable**. Work is not always going to be about fun and games. Your coworkers or managers may not like you, and that's okay. It's actually to be expected, especially if people feel threatened by you. Remember that you are getting paid to do your job. Do it and take your ass home!

**15. Stay in your lane**. Don't swerve all across the road. Mind *your* business. If you are minding someone else's business and worrying about his or her responsibilities, you will neglect your own.

**16. Network, network, network.** Make it a priority to stay in touch with your college friends and old coworkers. Join industry associations and build professional relationships with people in your field, so that you may foster a network of people who can help your career grow.

**17. Pay attention to the small things**. Lots of people are intelligent, diligent, and perform well at work. But it's the ones who pay attention to detail who truly stand out in the crowd. Reply to your work emails in a timely fashion, send thank-you notes to your boss and colleagues when appropriate, and show up on time for appointments. This attention to detail doesn't require much effort, but people will appreciate them more than you might think.

**18. Make a "to-do" list**. Keep a notebook with you at work. Before you check your emails, make a list of things that you need to do or accomplish for the day to keep you from forgetting something or being disorganized.

**19. Honor your work/life boundaries.** Don't be a slave to your job. If the president of the United States can find time for vacation, so can you. Take trips, leave work at a reasonable hour (at least on most days), and enjoy your weekends. If you don't set limits on the time you spend at your job, your boss won't either. See #13.

# Chapter 5:
## All About the Benjamins

Money always burned a hole in my daughter's pocket. I don't care if it's a dollar—if she has it, she has to spend it. When she started working, she would literally flush her money down the toilet. What I mean is that she was spending all of her hard-earned money on food. She was working to eat and she didn't have to; I cooked every night, so she was pissing away her money. It angered me. When my daughter started having lunch in Georgetown with her friends, I confirmed that she was living in La-La Land. I work full-time and cannot afford to have lunch in Georgetown every Saturday.

I tried everything to convince her that she had to change the way that she managed her money. It wasn't until she went to college that she understood. I began by giving her a monthly allowance and purchased the mandatory unlimited meal plan her freshman year. However, when I looked at her bank account I saw that all of her funds were being spent on food—that was it! That was the last straw. She could flush her money down the toilet if she wanted to, but this time, it was my money that was going down the drain. So I did the only thing that I felt I could do: I stopped giving her the allowance and she had to live off of the cafeteria food.

She had to struggle in order to finally appreciate having any money at all, and as a result, she has learned to be more frugal and does a better job with managing her money. Now, when I review her account, I no longer see Chipotle, McDonald's, or 7-Eleven on the list. Progress!

**1. Don't go broke trying to look rich.** Yeah, that $300 Michael Kors handbag looks appealing, but if you don't have any money in the bank, you should probably keep moving. Don't be a jackass trying to keep up with the Jones'. What's better? Money in your bank account or a $300 handbag with $10 in it?

**2. Act your wage.** Check yourself financially. If you don't have the money to pay for something, you don't need it. Never go in debt trying to keep up with everyone else.

**3. Your parents don't have a money tree in their back yard.** Be reasonable about what you ask for. You have no idea what your parents have to do for or with their money. If you are grown, you really shouldn't be asking your parents for shit.

**4. Live beneath your means.** Having champagne taste on a beer budget doesn't make any sense. Don't try to be someone that you can't afford to be.

**5. Recognize the difference between your wants and needs.** If something is not necessary for you to survive, it's a want, not a need.

**6. Always pay yourself first when you get paid.** Save at least 10% of your paycheck every time you get paid.

**7. Invest in your retirement.** Enroll in a 401k plan. If you ever leave your current job and work somewhere else, roll your 401k into the new employers' 401k plan. Do not withdraw the money.

**8. Save your coins.** Don't spend every dime you have. Unless are psychic, you cannot predict the future. If you could, you would know exactly how much money you would need in the future. So, save money for the future and unexpected emergencies. Open a savings and checking account. Do your research and decide which bank best fits your needs. If you have the opportunity to join a Credit Union, even better! Credit unions always have better interest rates.

**9. Pay attention to interest rates.** Would you dive in a pool without knowing how deep it is? No? Then why would you take out a loan without knowing the interest rates?

**10. Invest in real estate.** Investing in real estate is one of the few investment tools where using the bank's money couldn't be easier. The ability to make a down payment, leverage your capital, and increase your overall return on investment is incredible.

**11. Create a budget and stick to it.** Sticking to your budget will prevent you from overspending and putting yourself in a horrible financial situation. It's hard to pass up that new dress or not eating out when you don't feel like cooking, but it will be all worth it when you look at your bank account.

**12. Have a life insurance policy**. If you are an adult with a job, you should be able to purchase life insurance. Don't force your family to create a GoFUNDME campaign to pay for your funeral. It's embarrassing and distasteful. Compare rates and choose a policy that is best for you.

**13. Don't be a brand whore.** Sure, everyone likes named brand clothes, but don't pass up good quality products with a great price just because it doesn't have the right name. Who's going to see the tag anyway?

**14. Invest in the stock market.** If you keep your money under a mattress instead of investing it, it doesn't work for you and you will never have than what you save. By investing, you are getting your money to make more money for you.

**15. Learn to do a lot with a little.** If you can't manage a little bit of money, how do you expect to manage a lot of money? Making more money is not going to solve your problems if you have horrible spending habits.

# Chapter 6:
## Your Stankin' Ass

I don't think that girls wash their ass or brush their teeth from the ages of ten to thirteen. I'm not sure if it's a stage or what, but it's disgusting. There was a point when my daughter would literally smell like a five-pound bag of onions. I tried every deodorant known to man, but that onion smell would not go away. I would wash her clothes and her shirts would still smell of onions. I didn't get it. She was bathing every night (at least I thought she was), so I didn't understand why she would wake up smelling like she just participated in a triathlon. And she didn't get it! She thought that I was being mean and obsessive, but I know that kids are meaner than I am—I didn't want her to get teased at school.

It wasn't until I ran across a blog that suggested that armpit hair can be the cause of smells. I shaved her armpits and she's hasn't been musty since. Why didn't I think of that sooner?

Your mother may not know everything, but when she offers you advice about personal hygiene, try to be receptive. Trust me: she was once your age and her mother probably had those same conversations with her.

**1. It's only hair.** Seriously. You will curl it and straighten it and pull it back and pin it up. You'll wish it were thicker or longer or curlier or straighter. You'll braid, twist, and color (please, not purple). You'll spend countless hours making a fuss over your hair, but what's the use? It's *hair*. Life is too precious to waste so much time. Put it in a pony or put a hat on it, then go out and conquer the world.

**2. Be beautifully you.** You don't have to be accepted by others; you only have to be accepted by yourself. Learn to love yourself for who you are, not what others perceive you to be. Self-acceptance is liberating!

**3. Always look nice and neat when you leave the house.** Never leave the house looking like you don't give a fuck. If you do, then other people won't give a fuck about how they treat you or talk to you.

**4. Never wear a headscarf or pajama pants outside.** It's slack and you will look like a hood rat. See #3.

**5. Always iron your clothes.** It takes less than five minutes to iron your clothes. If you don't like ironing, get a steamer or take your clothes to the cleaners. Take pride in your appearance.

**6. Spend more time worrying about how beautiful you are on the inside than on the outside**. It's fine to take pride in your appearance and want to be flawless, but if you are only consumed with how you look, you'll pay for it eventually. Yes, you are beautiful, flawless even—but never forget that true beauty comes from being unselfish, kind, and compassionate. If you are dark and ugly on the inside, it doesn't matter how beautiful you look on the outside. You're butt ugly. Period.

**7. Don't get tatted up.** Personally, I think that everyone should be able to express themselves freely, but be smart about it. If you choose to have body art, be smart. Don't get a random picture of Daisy Duck on your leg or some man's name tattooed on your breast. What the hell are you going to do when you are thirty, forty, and fifty, when you become someone's mama, nana, or wife? Be very careful about long-term consequences.

**8. Don't dress like a whore.** It's wrong for people to judge you based on how you dress, but it happens. Trust me, looking like a $2 whore will get you the wrong kind of attention. Save yourself the trouble.

**9. Wash your ass!** It's that simple. If you can smell yourself, someone else can too, only they won't tell you. They will just talk about you behind your back.

**10. Drop the Soap!** Don't use soap to clean your phunk box. You can use soap to clean every other area of your body, but steer clear of the vagina. The chemicals will disturb your natural pH-balance, and might result in yeast infection (and trust me, you don't want a yeast infection).

**11. Wear clean clothes.** Do I have to explain why? Clean underwear and clothes are a must!

**12. Mow the lawn.** Pubic hair results in odor. Shave or wax periodically. The same goes for your underarms!

**13. Take your trash out.** Used sanitary napkins/tampons should be thrown out every day. Nothing smells worse than blood hitting the air.

**14. Wash your hair on a regular basis.** The skin on your scalp is just like the skin on your body: it has oil and sweat glands, which produce natural-occurring bacteria that can cause—you guessed it—odor.

**15. Air it out.** Let your phunk box get some air. Try going without panties when you go to bed. When there's no airflow to the vagina, bacteria and fungi can collect and grow in the moist, dark folds, which, again, may cause yeast infections. Letting it all air out can regulate downtown moisture and prevent yeast infections.

**16. Cotton in the summer.** Wear white cotton panties in the summer. If you think you're a Victoria's Secret model and you don't own cotton panties, opt for panty liners. Same deal.

**17. If you smell fish…** Something isn't right. Feminine sprays, deodorants, and perfumes may cover up the scent, but can't make it go away. If you have an abnormally strong or fishy scent, it is most likely a sign that you have an infection like bacterial vaginitis. If this is the case, only antibiotics will clear up the problem. Run to your gynecologist!

# Chapter 7:
## An Apple a Day

I never wanted my children to be embarrassed of me because of my weight, so for some time, I have been obsessed with dieting and working out. Over the years, I've watched my weight fluctuate. I would lose weight then gain it back and then lose it again. I was on a never-ending rollercoaster, because I was not doing the right things. I was so focused on how I looked on the outside that I failed to realize how my perception of myself was affecting my daughter.

At the age of ten, Sejal began to express how terrified she was of being overweight. She had to be all of seventy pounds at the time. I knew then that I had to change her perception of being healthy and fit. I had to first love the skin that I was in. So, I stopped complaining about every flaw and embraced who I was and what my body looked like. I ate healthy and prepared nutritious meals for my family. I changed my perception of what health and beauty meant to me. If I was unhappy with the way I looked, that was between me, myself, and my mirror. It's still a work in progress, but I think my daughter has taken notice. She now compliments me and tells me that I am beautiful just the way I am. And so is she.

**1. Life is more fun when you're fit.** When you are physically fit, you can enjoy almost everything in sports and life. Not to mention you will look good in your jeans.

**2. Eat clean and healthy (organic if you can afford it).** Healthy and fresh eating is important. When you eat clean you are in better moods, sleep sounder, have more energy, have flawless skin, and have improved brain function.

**3. Work out for at least thirty minutes daily.** Any kind of cardio activity increases your BPM (heartbeats per minute), which increases blood flow to working muscles. Experts believe that as little as thirty minutes of cardio three to five days a week will add six years to your life. When you're physically active, something happens to your spirit and mind. You literally glow. Who doesn't love a natural glow?

**4. Moisturize, moisturize, moisturize!** It's never too early to start preventing wrinkles.

**5. Screw the stilettos.** They look cute, but such high heels strain the joints from your toes all the way up to your lower back and can cause bunions and hammertoes. If you must wear them, wear flats first then change into your stilettos when you get where you're going. Your feet will thank you later.

**6. Get at least eight hours of sleep at night.** Studies show that if you get at least eight hours of sleep, you will get sick less often, maintain a healthy weight, lower your risk of high blood pressure and diabetes, reduce stress and improve your mood, think more clearly, and get along better with people.

**7. Get annual checkups.** You have one body, so take cake care of it! See your primary physician at least once a year to make sure you are healthy.

**8. Don't Diet. Make lifestyle changes.** Diets will temporarily take the weight off, but often results in gaining the weight you lost and then some. If you want long-term results, you have to change your overall eating habits.

**9. Take care of your skin and hair.** If you can afford to, get regular facials and visit your favorite salon at least twice a month. Your skin and hair will thank you.

**10. Manage your weight.** I know, I know: all women hate scales, but get one anyway. One of the most effective ways to maintain your weight is to monitor your weight at least twice a week.

**11. Your ultimate goal shouldn't be to look fit, it should be to be fit.** Looking good in your clothes is great, but if you are torn up from the floor up health-wise, let's see how good you look at thirty, forty, or fifty. Visual fitness is always more impressive and something people can judge instantly, up until the moment when you have to run or perform physical tasks. Endurance, strength and flexibility can't be achieved by looking good.

**12. Run like you stole something.** You don't have to be a marathon runner to reap the benefits of running. Running will make your life better, as well as make you more confident, braver, and tougher. A healthy mind is just as important as a healthy body. When you run, your body releases endorphins, sparking the growth of new nerve cells. This increases the volume of oxygen flow to your brain which improves learning and memory.

**13. Take care of your body—it's the only one you have.** Be cognizant of what you put into your body. Care for yourself by focusing less on what you put on the outside of your body and more on what you put inside it. Being reckless when you are young will catch up with you when you are older.

**14. When you turn forty, get a mammogram.** Mammograms don't prevent breast cancer, but they can save lives by finding early signs. Finding breast cancers in the initial stages has helped many women to seek treatment more quickly and to keep their breasts. When caught early, localized cancers can be removed without resorting to breast removal (mastectomy).

**15. Listen to your body.** If it's singing a bad tune, you may need a tune up. See #7

**16. See your gynecologist.** Please get annual PAP Smears, especially if you are sexually active. If you don't take care of your phunk box, who will?

**17. Zip It!** Dust off your old prom dress and try it on. If the zipper doesn't budge past your ribs, you could be at an increased risk for breast cancer. Recent American Cancer Society studies show that women who had gained twenty-one to thirty pounds after age eighteen were 40 percent more likely to develop the disease than those who didn't put on more than five pounds. Women who gained seventy or more pounds doubled their risk.

# Chapter 8:
## Do Unto Others

By the time my daughter was in high school, I noticed a change in her attitude. She was still the sweet girl that I raised, but she was also a "mean girl," just like from the box office movie. I watched how she treated people: she was nice to people that she liked, but God help you if she didn't like you! I didn't know if it was a phase or what, but I didn't like it.

I encouraged her to try counseling, but she refused to go. I tried leading by example, but that didn't work. So, I decided to treat her exactly the way she treated me. If she was mean or disrespectful, I would give it right back to her. If she didn't answer my texts or calls, I would do the same to her (especially when I knew she needed something). I would even go as far as to block her calls and texts.

Needless to say, she did not like being treated the way that she did others and me. After a couple of months, it finally sunk in that she couldn't be mean and disrespectful to me and not suffer consequences. Her attitude has improved, but every now and then when the "mean girl" reappears, what's done unto her is exactly what she does unto others.

**1. You don't *always* have to take the high road.** Not everyone deserves it. Sometimes someone's actions and words warrant you giving them exactly what they are asking for. It will make you feel better.

**2. Learn what you are willing to accept, what you really need, and when and how to let go.** You don't have to put up with anyone's shit. If you don't like how someone is treating you, remove yourself from the situation. If you choose to stay, take responsibility and don't complain about it to others.

**3. Invest your time and energy into people and activities that add value to your life.** Fly with the eagles or cluck with the hens. Keep positive people in your circle. Stay away from simple people. Stupidity is contagious.

**4. When people show you who they are, believe them.** In every relationship whether romantic, platonic, business, or family, people will show you who they truly are. If someone tells you that they don't like you, believe them. If they say that they don't care, believe them. If they ignore you, purposely hurt you, or are careless with your feelings, believe them the first time it happens. Pay attention. Don't let someone show you who they are more than once.

**5. Don't be afraid of speaking your mind.** Never be scared or worried that you will disappoint your parents, partners, or friends. Be afraid of being a disappointment to yourself. Stand firm in your beliefs and say something!

**6. Always be kind.** Everyone you meet is dealing with issues that you know nothing about and that's not your business, but be kind and compassionate. You never know what someone else is going through.

**7. Never expect anything from anyone and you will never be disappointed.** People will disappoint you, so don't expect them to do what you know they aren't able to deliver. For instance, if you know someone is incapable of being honest, don't expect them to tell you the truth.

**8. Always look people in the eye when you talk to them.** The easiest explanation to why we should make eye contact, and lots of it, is because it shows the person that you're talking to that they are the center of your attention. And who doesn't love being the center of attention?

**9. Don't give anyone any ammunition against you.** Your business is just that: *your* business. Keep what you are doing to yourself and you will never have to worry about it being in the street.

**10. Never be careless with someone else's feelings.** Don't hurt someone's feelings trying to make a point. It won't make you or the other person feel good. Even if it makes you feel better for a while, it won't be worth it in the end.

**11. What you do to others will come back to you.** You better believe that what you put out in the universe, whether positive or negative, will come back to you. Always do right by people, because Karma is a bitch!

**12. No one is perfect and that includes you.** Stop expecting perfection from others. Unless you are God (and you are not), you will make mistakes. Don't expect anyone else not to make them. We are all living to learn.

**13. Always be who you are no matter who you're around.** If people can't accept you for who you are, fuck 'em! Always be true to who you are.

**14. If someone doesn't like you, that's *their* problem.** Everyone is not going to like you and that's ok.

**15. Someone else's opinion of you is none of your business.** Stop worrying about what other people think about you. What matters is what you think of yourself.

**16. Never give anyone enough power to determine whether you are happy or sad.** You determine your happiness. No one should have so much control over your emotions that they influence what kind of day you're having. If they do, they are toxic. Detox ASAP!

**17. People are not always meant to be in your life forever.** Just because someone is in your life now does not mean that they are meant to stay forever. Sometimes they are in your life long enough to teach you lessons that you need to learn.

Don't be afraid to let them go.

**18. It's perfectly ok to rid yourself of toxic relationships.** Detox periodically! See #2 and #17.

**19. It's okay to trust people, but don't be anyone's fool.** Don't be afraid to trust someone, but always watch your back.

**20. Don't judge anyone—only God can judge.** It's in the Bible! Besides, judging a person does not define who they are; it defines who you are.

**21. It's not always necessary to call people out on their bullshit.** Nine times out of ten, *they* know that you know that they are full of it.

**22. Your value does not decrease based on someone else's inability to see your worth.** How someone else perceives you should not define who you are. Know your own worth!

**23. Sometimes you've got to give up on people.** Not because you don't care, but because they don't.

**24. Don't depend on anyone to do anything for you that you can do for yourself.** Never count on someone else to handle your business. No one handles your business like you can, so take care of your own shit or be disappointed when someone lets you down. You choose.

**25.** *You* **teach people how to treat you.** Determine what is or isn't acceptable to you and stick to it. No one is going to do more than you allow them to do.

# Chapter 9:
## La Familia

No matter how much your family gets on your nerves, there is nothing you can do about who your family members are. There are family members that you can't stand and then there are those you love and will always have a close relationship with. My daughter has her Aunt T. They have always been as thick as thieves—Aunt T has spoiled her rotten and Sejal has loved every minute of it.

When Sejal was about five-years-old, her Aunt T was diagnosed with fibromyalgia. She had a hard time adjusting and, as a result, had low self-esteem. At five, my daughter was already mature and outspoken. I guess at some point, she was tired of her Aunt's constant crying and complaining. One day, I overheard her tell her Aunt T, "Look, you need to get up and do things for yourself and stop crying and complaining about it. What is crying going to do?"

Now, I certainly don't condone disrespectful behavior, but in this situation, tough love was very necessary. Aunt T was working my nerves too. But that's family for you: they will check you, fight you, talk about you, chastise you, but they are still family. Sometimes receiving advice from family members is hard, but necessary. Like it or not, you're stuck with them!

**1. Family comes first.** No matter what. Nothing is more important than family.

**2. Sometimes your family will be your biggest critics.** They will be harder on you than people in the street. It's either because they love you or because they are jealous of you. Figure out which it is and you'll know how to deal with them.

**3. Always honor your mother and father…the Bible says so!** Always respect your parents, even when you think they are acting stupid and don't know anything. You can think all kinds of disrespectful things in your head, but they better not come out of your mouth!

**4. Other things may change, but our beginning and ending is family**. Your family will always be there through the good and bad.

**5. Families are like brownies: mostly sweet but every now and then you'll run across a nut.** Everyone has a crazy family member so you aren't alone.

**6. There's family and then there are relatives.** Know the difference. Family members are those who you have a close relationship with. Relatives are estranged family members who should stay relatively far away from, because, although you're related, they will be the first to stab you in the back.

**7. Sometimes your family will be the first to disappoint you.** You'll find that it is those who are close to you that may hurt you the most. It's perfectly all right to still love them—they're family! You can love them from a distance.

**8. You don't have to take crap from anyone not even family members.** Just because they are family doesn't mean that they have the right to say and do whatever they want to you. You do not have to be subject to their abuse.

**9. Learn how to love from a distance.** Every now and then you will come across a family member who doesn't mean you any good. Stay as far away from them as possible.

**10. No family is perfect.** You will argue, fight, and even stop talking to one another, but in the end, family is family and the love will always be there.

**11. You cannot choose your family but you can choose not to take their calls.** You don't have to pick up the phone every time someone who you don't want to talk to calls. If they are negative or want to call only to talk about the latest family gossip, don't answer the phone. You don't need any of that negativity.

**12. Family is not always about blood.** It's about who is there for you when you need them most.

**13. Remember, as far as people in the street know, you have a nice, functional family.** Keep your dysfunctional family business within the family.

**14. Family members are like the branches on a tree.** We all have the same roots, but sometimes, life takes us in different directions and that's perfectly fine.

**15. Just relax and enjoy the crazy.** Don't get caught up in who has what issues. All of us have our own struggles. Enjoy the time that you get to spend with family and make lasting memories.

**16. Be there for your family if you are in the position to do so.** No matter what you've achieved in life or done for humanity, if you haven't done anything for your family in their time of need, you haven't accomplished anything.

# Chapter 10:
# Friend or Foe?

Friends come a dime a dozen. They come and they go. It's hard to think that the person that you trust will ever betray you, but they can and will. Mothers can be great judges of character, so when my daughter once came home with a new "BFF," I knew instantly that there was something up with her. She seemed sneaky and conniving. I advised my daughter to watch her back and not to trust everyone. Needless to say, I was right. Not only had her "BFF" spread mean rumors about her, she also tried to sleep with her boyfriend. My daughter was devastated. She couldn't believe that her "friend" would betray her. She was hurt beyond measure and I felt helpless. I wanted to relieve her of the pain she felt. I knew all along that her friend was trouble, but still, I didn't say, "I told you so." I just held Sejal in my arms and reassured her that things would be okay. Sometimes, it's the people who are the closest to you that will hurt you the most. There is a thin line between a friend and foe.

**1. Everyone is not your friend.** Not everyone who says they are your friend is actually looking out for you. Actions always speak louder than words.

**2. Some girls are just mean girls.** Be careful when you choose your friends. Girls can be petty, nasty, cruel, and jealous. Some of them pretend to be your friend and stab you in the back, and will cut you deep. If you're unprepared for the inevitable, it will crush you even more.

**3. Friends are lifesavers.** When you find a loyal, true friend, hold onto her. Boys will come and go, but a good girlfriend will be there for you through the mountains, valleys, and everything in between.

**4. Be the friend that you want others to be to you.** If you are going to be someone's friend, be a true one. Think of how you want your friend to treat you. If you are anything less than what you imagine, then you need to work on it.

**5. There is a difference between a friend and an associate.** A true friend is someone who is down for you in your darkest hours. An associate is someone who's cool to hang out with, but is not really interested in what goes on with you. Unfortunately, sometimes a person you consider a friend is actually just an associate. A friend reciprocates your kindness; if you have her back, she'll have yours. If you pay for lunch, she's got you the next time you are out. Associates are takers; they take your kindness for weakness. If you are always being a giver and never get anything in return, you are probably dealing with an associate and not a ride-or-die friend.

**6. Don't be a hater.** Your light will shine brighter when you don't blow someone else's light out. There is room for everyone to shine. Always uplift, love, and encourage your friends.

**7. Don't be cliquish.** Have friends of different cultures and all walks of life. Being in a clique is boring. The fun begins when you take the lid off of the box.

**8. You are who you hang around.** If you surround yourself with stupid people with no moral values, eventually, you'll be just like them.

**9. It's okay to share your friend.** You are not her/his only friend. Don't be jealous when she/he has other friends. That doesn't mean that they aren't your friend or don't love you. Just know that every relationship is different and has its own special meaning.

# Chapter 11:
## The World is Yours

By the time I was in high school, I had lived in different countries and visited exotic places all around the world. I have seen and done a lot and enjoyed every minute of it.

I know plenty of people who dream of visiting other countries, but let life get in the way. There's a big world out there! Why be complacent in the bubble that you're in? There is so much that can be learned about other countries and cultures. Life is short, so you should explore as often as you can. Meeting people from exotic cultures will teach you that the way you view the world or the way that media portrays things is not totally accurate.

Experience things for yourself, so that you have different perspectives on life and become a well-rounded person. Be open and free to live life and enjoy this beautiful world that God created.

**1. Be open to new experiences.** Don't be afraid to try new things. Don't limit yourself because of fear of the unknown. Just climb the damn mountain already!

**2. When you have free time go to a museum.** Most museums are free and packed with a lot of history. Discovering new things is always exciting.

**3. Attend a concert.** When your favorite artist is in town, spend the money and go see them. It'll be an experience that you won't forget.

**4. There's no guarantee that you'll live to be 100**. Live in the moment. Traveling is often postponed with the intentions of doing it later in life. Choose to buy experiences over materialistic things. Traveling will be the best investment that you'll ever make. Climb mountains, walk treks, ride waves. And try doing these things in other countries!

**5. Get up and Go.** As often as you can to wherever you can. Never pass up an opportunity to experience somewhere new, even if it's just two blocks away.

**6. Take pictures.** Always. They will last forever.

**7. A smile is universal.** Try it. No matter where you are from or where you are going, a smile means the same thing. You appear more approachable and who knows? You may make a new friend.

**8. Don't be obsessed with planning**. It's okay to plan, but leave your schedule open. Throw out the itinerary and just have a few basics in place: flights and accommodations with a short list of activities in your destination. The more flexible you are, the more fun you will have.

**9. Who needs a diploma?** Let the world be your institute for higher learning. Traveling is one of the best educations that money can buy.

**10. Be fearless, but cautious.** Don't be afraid to let your hair down and try it all. Just be careful.

**11. Home is where the heart is.** Home is not a place—it's more of a feeling. Make a home for yourself inside your heart. Find what you need to make it comfortable, whether it be great friends, love, lasting memories, or all of the above. That way home will be wherever you are.

**12. Things will go wrong.** Delayed flights, lost luggage, missed excursions, poor weather. Traveling is the ultimate test of character when the going gets rough. Go with the flow. You will alleviate so much unnecessary stress.

**13. Let go of your expectations and keep yourself open to any and all possibilities.** That way you will be pleasantly surprised when things go splendid and never disappointed if they fall flat.

# Chapter 12:
## Safe and Secure

Your mother can never talk to you enough about being safe. She knows that you're not her little princess anymore: yesterday, you were playing with dolls, now you're wearing miniskirts and hanging out with your friends. She's wondering where the time went. Unfortunately, she can't make you wear a sign that reads, "I know that I look 20, but I'm only 15." What a better place the world would be if that could happen?

The truth is that there are some real freak shows out there. You see them on the news every day: men and women who want nothing more than to exploit you, sexually, physically, and emotionally. So how do you prepare for that? Even when mothers teach our daughters to stay away from strangers, statistics show that you are more likely to be assaulted by someone that you know. It's critical that you are careful about the people you let in your circle and pay attention to your surroundings. Doing so will help thwart potential dangers.

**1. Never walk alone at night.** If walking by yourself, get off your cell phone. Many people think that being on the phone is safe, because the person on the other line can call 911, but that rarely works out. Chatting can distract you; it's better to be aware of your surroundings.

**2. Pay Attention.** Be aware of what's going on around you, who's around, and what they are doing. Be ready to respond if you need to.

**3. Prepare before you leave.** Have your keys in your hand before you make it to your car or when you are leaving your car to enter your house; that way, you aren't fumbling in your purse or pockets. Be ready to get in your car fast so that you can lock your doors.

**4. Don't tell people where you live.** If you are going on a first, second, or even third date, meet them at the location or get picked up from a public place. People you aren't close friends with should not know where you live.

**5. Always invest in an alarm system.** Yeah, it's another bill, but it will give you security. Homes without security systems are 2.7 times more likely to be targeted by a burglar. The mere presence of an alarm system is enough in most cases to protect the home and its occupants from break-ins.

**6. Check your car before you get in it.** Look in your backseat, underneath, and around your car before you get in it.

**7. Don't accept drinks that are given to you.** Never accept a drink that has been sent over to you. If someone wants to buy you a drink, walk to the bar with them and watch the bartender make it. Always pour your own drink at a party and take it with you everywhere, even to the bathroom. This will make it a lot harder for someone to drug you via a drink.

**8. Use the Buddy System.** When going out with your girlfriends, agree that you will stick together. Do not let your friend go off alone with a dude.

**9. Never put your name on your apartment buzzer.** If you're expecting guests, just let them know which number to push. This way, only particular people know exactly where you live.

**10. If someone you know hurts you, tell someone.** Studies show that most women are physically and sexually assaulted by someone they know. Be weary of who you trust. If something doesn't feel right, then nine times out of ten, it isn't. And if someone you know does hurt you, tell someone! Report to the police. Never be silent.

**11. Take defense classes.** Always be prepared to protect and defend yourself.

**12. Never give anyone access to your house keys.** Mechanics seems harmless, right? Wrong! Assume that everyone can be a potential threat to you. When getting your car serviced, always remove your house keys and only provide the key needed to operate the vehicle.

**13. Make eye contact.** Always look straight into the face of potential enemies. Eye contact may scare off attackers, because they fear you will be able to identify them.

**14. Throw being nice out of the window.** Women tend to be sympathetic—forget that! Predators play on the sympathies of unsuspecting women to lure them into dangerous situations. If someone asks for directions, the time, directions, or help with their car, be polite but keep it moving.

**15. Switch up your routine.** Don't do the exact same thing every day. Regularly change your routine. No one should be able to tell when you are going to do anything.

**16. Be suspicious and paranoid.** It is always better to be safe than sorry. When in a parking lot, look at the cars parked on both sides of your vehicle. If a man is sitting alone in the seat closest to your car or if you are parked next to a van, always enter your car from the opposite side. If the parking lot or garage is dark or deserted, go back and find a friend or guard who can walk you to your car. Avoid any potential threats whenever possible, which goes for people that you know as well. If you feel that something isn't right, get the hell out of there! And never be afraid to tell someone.

**17. Kick 'em in the nuts!** Hit an attacker where it hurts. The groin, eyes, knees and throat are vulnerable and effective places to kick and gouge.

# Chapter 13:
## Let's Talk About Sex

When my daughter was six, I gave it to her straight, no chaser. I know what you're saying: you talked to your daughter about sex when she was six?! Yes, indeed, I did. Apparently, other kids were talking about it at school, which made her curious. I can't say that it was an easy conversation to have, but it was necessary. I told her that she shouldn't just give it away to anyone and explained why she should remain a virgin until she was married. On that day, we made a deal that whenever she felt that she was "ready," she would talk to me first. I was hoping that by talking to me first I would be able to convince her to abstain.

It wasn't until she was sixteen that I realized she had broken our pact. I was heartbroken and my feelings were hurt. She promised me! I couldn't look at her for weeks and I felt like I lost my best friend. Although I did not handle her news well, I eventually stopped feeling like I had failed and appreciated the fact that she told me at all. She really didn't have to tell me anything. I was glad that I could put my personal feelings aside and be there for her. I didn't judge or scold her, so she opened up even more. Now she talks to be about everything (well, not *everything*. I can't handle *everything*). Right now, I am just happy that we have some sort of dialogue about sex and everything that comes with it.

Your mother will be a great person to talk to if you have questions about sex. It may be uncomfortable for both of you, but in the end, it'll be worth the conversation. Your mother (whether she wants to admit it or not) has been exactly where you are. Who better to go to for advice?

**1. It's okay to wait.** Guys are going try to sell you the world to get in your drawers. Don't believe them. Don't let anyone pressure you into having sex. If you don't want to do it, don't! It's your decision, but remember that once you give it away, you can't get it back. No one ever regrets taking things slow, but a lot of girls do regret rushing.

**2. Masturbate.** Some of the best sex you'll have will be with yourself. Spend time on your own playing around and finding out what works for you too. Not to mention it's safe.

**3. Orgasms are brilliant.** It doesn't matter how you get there, so long as you get there.

**4. Say what you like.** Don't hesitate to say what you like and what you don't like when it comes to sex. Men like smart, strong, loud, funny women. At least, all the men worth bothering with.

**5. It's yours.** Your sexuality is not a "gift" that you have to hang onto and give to somebody. It's yours. Always was, always will be.

**6. Porn is just someone's fantasy**. Don't take it seriously.

**7. Sex can be fun.** It's even more fun when done safely and with a person you care about and trust.

**8. Have standards.** Hold yourself and your sexuality to higher standards and choose not to just give it away to anybody.

**9. Learn as you go.** We are overwhelmed with mixed messages about how to perform sexuality. We go into experiences with a lot of curiosity and little to no guidance, all of which can lead to strange concepts about what sex is or what we're supposed to get out of it, or why we're even doing it at all. There's no manual for having a happy and healthy sex life. Figure out what works for you and what doesn't, then go from there.

**10. Consider why you're doing it.** Sex is exciting. And it feels good. These are reasons enough for being curious, but you must know who you are and know your worth. If you're having sex, because you want someone to like you or think you're cool, you're way off track. What matters is knowing *your* state of mind, *your* level of comfort, and *your* own reasoning. It will take time to figure things out, but that's all a part of it.

**11. Don't be reckless.** Mistakes come at a high cost. Choosing the wrong partner or choosing to have multiple partners than you are truly comfortable with can wreak havoc on your self-esteem.

**12. Consider your self-worth to be as important as contraception.** Loving yourself and having a sense of self-worth will assist you in making healthy decisions when choosing partners. The goal is to enjoy sex, not to use it as a placeholder for unresolved emotional or personal issues you may have. There are consequences for being irresponsible and there are always other ways to feel better than giving it up.

**13. Your body was designed to give you pleasure.** It's a proven scientific fact: your clitoris does not serve any other purpose.

**14. Use protection.** Always. It will protect you from venereal diseases and pregnancy. Some guys will make up every excuse in the world not to use protection. I don't care if he says he's allergic to condoms: tell him your phunk box is allergic to dumb dick.

**15. You can't phuck the world.** There are double standards when it comes to men and women and their sexuality. It's okay for men to have multiple partners, but if a woman does, she is viewed as a whore. It's not fair, it's not right, but it's life. No one is going to buy a car with a lot of miles on it. The value is depreciated and the more miles you have, the more you lose value.

**16. Get tested.** Before you have sex with anyone, get tested and require that your partner gets tested as well. It's important that you know your status and the status of your partners.

# Chapter 14:
## Men Are from Mars

I've always tried to prepare my daughter for relationships with the opposite sex. I always wanted her to be comfortable with who she was, so she wouldn't settle for anyone. When my daughter was in the fourth grade she burst through the door after school, announcing that some little boy at school said that she was his "Baby Mama." She thought it was funny, almost like she was honored that he chose her to hold such a title. I, on the other hand, did not think it was cute. I thought to myself, that times have surely changed. Were little boys skipping past liking someone and having a girlfriend, and going straight to Baby Mama?

After talking to her, I broke down what a Baby Mama was. I explained to her that, sometimes, circumstances will put one in a position to be a Baby Mama. I was one at a point in my life, but I wanted better for Sejal. I wanted her to choose a different path that included dating, love, and holding the title of "Wife." I wanted to make sure that I always poured into my daughter so that she knew she was loved. It was important to me that she knew her worth, so that she wouldn't settle for

DR. TAMMY JAMESON

empty compliments and promises. I wanted her to be smarter than I was when dealing with men. Men are from Mars, but they aren't that hard to figure out.

**1. Assume that every man you meet wants some ass.** Now, that doesn't mean that every man you meet is going to try you, and it also doesn't mean that sex is all men are going to want from you. There are going to be men who want to have real conversations with you, spend all of their time with you, learn everything they can about you, and wake up next to you for the rest of your life. Just remember that men wanting to get some ass may be the base. Don't forget it.

**2. Most men will take what they can get.** Don't be naïve and think that just because they love you and care about you that they wouldn't cheat on you in a second.

**3. When in doubt, break up.** If things aren't going the way they should, and you know in your heart that you're dealing with a loser, break up. Don't get stuck in a relationship that's going nowhere.

**4. Relationship drama is for grown people.** If you're nineteen years old and you and your boyfriend have constant drama, break up with him. You're too young to be working anything out if you aren't even old enough to drink. Life is too short.

• 86 •

**5. Don't try to save him.** I know it sounds cold-blooded, but you don't have time to be saving a man. You should be enjoying life and having fun, not babysitting a man who is depressed with low self-esteem. He needs a therapist, not a girlfriend.

**6. Let him prove himself to you.** Never try to prove that you're good enough for anyone. It should be the other way around.

**7. Never take care of a man.** What are you his momma? Once you start, he will always expect you to do things. If he can't take care of himself, what the hell do you need him for?

**8. Carry yourself like a queen.** Do so and you will attract a king, not a boy. You get what you put out in the universe. If you carry yourself like a hoe, don't be surprised when you attract nothing but losers.

**9. You are more than a booty call.** Conduct yourself accordingly. If a man only wants to see you in the wee hours of the morning or doesn't want to be seen in public with you, he doesn't want to eat with you. He wants to sleep with you.

**10. He should look out for you.** If he drops you off and doesn't wait until you get in the house before he burns rubber, tell him to kick rocks. He doesn't give a damn about you or your safety.

**11. Never tell a man what to do.** He should be able to make his own decisions. You're not his mother. Besides, a man is going to do what he wants to do regardless.

**12. Never let a man tell you more than once that he doesn't want you.** When he tells you he doesn't want to be with you, believe him. You deserve whatever you get if you continue to pursue a relationship with someone who isn't interested in you. And don't get it confused: he will still sleep with you even though he doesn't want a relationship with you. Don't get caught up.

**13. You don't have to show your teeth to every man you meet.** You don't have to be in every man's face. Keep it business and keep it moving.

**14. Never be up in a married man's face.** It's disrespectful whether your intentions are innocent or not. If you need something from him, show respect and go through his wife.

**15. Keep your legs closed.** Every Tom, Dick, Harry, and Dontae does not need to know what your phunk box looks like. Have some self-respect.

**16. Men, you can live with them.** But if he's a total loser, it's perfectly fine to leave his ass right where you found him.

**17. Never run after a man.** If he wants to be with you, he'll chase you. Never desperately pursue anyone; love will arrive when it's ready, so don't sabotage things with impatience. Running behind someone who doesn't want to be caught will impair your dignity and hurt your chances of finding someone great. When things are the other way around, you look desperate and needy. Actually, you look more like a psycho chick. He'll run like hell!

**18. Your father is not your man.** And there it is! Once you reach a certain age, it is not your father's responsibility to get your hair and nails done or to pay your bills. Stop trying to hustle your dad like he's some dude off of the street. Take care of yourself!

# Chapter 15:
## If He Hits You

My first husband was an abuser. Deep inside, I knew that before I ever married him. I saw the signs, but I ignored them, because I thought that I could change him. I was wrong. I met him when I was nineteen: young, free, and enjoying life.

Slowly, but surely, I allowed him to change who I was. Piece by piece, he broke me down. He started by alienating me from my friends. According to him, there was something was wrong with all of them and thus, he hated them. In the beginning, I still did what I wanted to and just listened to his mouth later. Eventually, I didn't want to hear his mouth, so I started making up excuses to tell my friends as to as why I didn't want to hang out. I passed up opportunity after opportunity, because I thought it would please him, only he would turn around and hang out all night with his friends. He was playing mind games. I didn't see it at the time.

After dating him for four years, I became pregnant with Sejal. I thought surely that he would change then. When he didn't, things got worse; he became verbally and physically abusive. Still, I stayed. I stayed three years after that and married him. By then, I was a hermit. I wasn't myself: I never smiled or laughed and I was miserable. My life was nothing like I envisioned it would be. Still, the abuse continued and I felt stuck. I knew that what I was experiencing was not love, but I didn't know how to change my situation.

When my daughter was in the second grade, I was in the bathroom helping her get ready for school. My ex-husband came in the bathroom and picked a fight with me, which resulted in me getting a cut on my face. He did all of this in front of our daughter: He didn't care about how it would affect her. He didn't care that she had testing at school that day. He just didn't care. Until that moment, I never stopped to think about how the arguments, demeaning comments, or physical abuse affected my daughter. What kind of example was I setting? If I tolerated abuse, then she would surely grow up and have similar experiences. I wanted more for her. I wanted more for myself.

It took me a few years after that incident, but I eventually packed up my things, my two kids, and a few pictures, and I left. I walked away from it all. I didn't want the house or anything that was in it. I just wanted peace. I divorced that coward and have been living in peace and happiness ever since. Every now and then, I will have a conversation with my daughter about the things she saw and heard. I want her to understand that our experiences were not normal and that, if anyone ever abuses her, she must walk away, because it won't get better. I was able to live long enough to get away. A lot of women are not that fortunate.

Abuse is never acceptable. If you are being abused get help. Love yourself enough to want better.

**1. Domestic violence is not just physical.** Abuse comes in many forms: physical, emotional, sexual, and mental. Don't accept any form of abuse from anyone.

**2. If he loves you, he won't hurt you.** Point blank, period.

**3. If a man puts his hands on you, get your shit and go.** Do not look back. If you let him get away with it once, he will do it again.

**4. Press charges.** He will cry and provide every reason under the sun as to why he abused you and that he will never do it again. That's bullshit. The only way he will truly be sorry is if you seek justice.

**5. Do not drop the charges.** So many women fall victim to domestic violence over and over again, because they let the abuser off the hook. You will only be hurting yourself.

**6. Realize that he isn't the one.** Any man who physically, emotionally, or spiritually abuses you is not the one—trust me!

**7. Always know that you are strong and confident.** Don't let someone else's actions change how you feel about yourself.

**8. Watch for red flags.** If your partner is showing you that he can potentially be an abuser, more than likely his behavior will get worse before it gets better. Pay attention to the signs: controlling behavior, bad temper, and emotional abuse. Stay as far away from him as possible. If he refuses to leave you alone, obtain a restraining order.

**9. Familiarize yourself with the cycle of violence**. There's a pattern or cycle of violence that is prevalent in abusive relationships. It begins with "the escalating phase" (demonstrated by anger, arguing, blaming, controlling); transfers to "the violent phase" (where the victim is physically attacked); then to "the making-up phase" (where the abuser cries, begs for forgiveness, vows to change, etc.). This cycle continues once the victim allows the abuser back in her life. Don't get trapped in the cycle. Pay attention to the signs.

**10. Support a friend or family member who is a victim of domestic violence.** If you know or suspect that a family member, friend, or work colleague is experiencing domestic violence, it may be difficult to know what to do, not to mention very upsetting that someone is hurting a person who you care about. Your first instinct may be to want to protect your friend or family member, but intervening can be dangerous for both you and her. Of course, this does not mean you should ignore it—seek help through outside sources like the police.

**11. Abuse is never okay.** If you or someone you know is in an abusive relationship, or if you have questions about domestic violence, contact the National Domestic Violence Hotline at 1-800-799-7233.

# Chapter 16:
# Love and Marriage,
# Love and Marriage

L ove is a beautiful thing. What's better than loving some-one who loves you just as much? While that may be, there will also be times when you love someone more than they love you. It sucks, but if you're strong, you will realize that the person is not for you and move on. It wasn't until I learned to love myself that I was able to truly receive love. Real love.

Think about it: how in the world can you love someone if you don't love and respect yourself? If you don't love yourself, why would you *think* that anyone would event *want* to love you? At the age of 39, I married the man that God created for me—it took me that long to get it. Up until I met him, I never knew that love could be drama-free. I didn't know that loving some-one didn't have to result in hurt and disappointment. My hus-band is the epitome of what God's vision of love is for me. He is my lover and my friend. I always respect him and show him in words and deeds that he is loved—I never want him to wonder.

I realize that husbands and wives have roles in their relationship. I know my role as a wife so I play my position. I don't swerve into his lane. I let him be what God created him to be: a leader and the head of our household. Some women simply want to run the house, their man, and their marriage, but love and marriage are not about control: it's about losing control. It's about trusting your partner to make decisions that are the best for you and your family. It's about letting someone else take the wheel and drive for once.

My daughter always tells me that she admires the marriage that my husband and I have. I've been so blessed to be able to show my children that marriage is about love, respect, trust and commitment. When and if my daughter decides to get married, I want her to have a happy and healthy marriage, and it's important to me that she realizes that such relationships begin with her.

**1. Love yourself first.** It is impossible to please everyone. Not everyone is going to love you and that's okay. Start with liking yourself: once you are comfortable with who you are it won't matter what others think. You can't expect anyone to love you if you don't love yourself.

**2. If you love, love with all of your heart.** If not, what's the point? Love with all you've got and if it doesn't work out, it doesn't work out.

**3. Always be open to receive love.** So you've been hurt a few times. I have too. It will happen, but there's growth in it all, so take it in and move on. Don't let hurt harden your heart. Love again and again and again until you find the person who God made for you.

**4. Never say "I Love you" if you don't mean it.** Don't ever lead someone on. Always be upfront and honest about how you feel. If you're "in like" and not "in love," say so. You'll save yourself a headache later.

**5. Don't test anyone.** Don't conduct periodic tests to make someone prove that they love you. Doing so only proves that you're afraid and insecure, and you may only end up disappointed. Then what?

**6. Learn to trust.** Trust yourself and the person you love. You were born with good instincts. Self-confidence fosters healthy relationships.

**7. Everyone doesn't express love the same.** Love is complicated and comes in all different shapes and forms. Some people express love differently than others. Who's to say that the way you show love is the way that everyone should? Don't assume love isn't there just because they don't reveal in ways you do or expect.

**8. Never lose yourself while loving someone else.** Always be true to who you are. If you can't love someone while being you and doing things that you love, then who are you?

**9. Love hurts sometimes.** Breakups can be painful, but nothing will teach you more about yourself than losing love.

**10. True love is about trust, compassion, generosity, and selflessness.** If any or all of these things aren't there in the relationship, neither should you.

**11. Be friends first.** Spend time nurturing a friendship with your partner and find interest in what interests him.

**12. You deserve to be loved.** Everyone does. Never let anyone make you feel any differently.

**13. A great marriage is a combination of many things.** It takes friendship, trust, respect, appreciation, admiration, and communication.

**14. Never let him wonder.** Tell him you love him and then show it with your actions.

**15. Spice it up.** Put on a wig. Be his whore. Do what you need to do to keep the fire burning.

**16. Be appreciative.** Always show gratitude by saying thank you and recognizing his effort. Say "Thank you" when he does things for you or for anything he buys you. Any money he gives you, even if it's for bills; anywhere he takes you—show appreciation and acknowledge his effort, because a simple "Thank you" goes a long way.

**17. Always be kind and sweet.** Never belittle him, especially in front of people or your children. Even if you think he's wrong, let him leave the room with his pride. A man without pride is broken. Watch how you talk to him and remember why you fell in love with him; reflect on those memories. It will help you through the tough times.

**19. Allow him to do his job**. A husband's job is to lead, provide, and protect you. Don't fight him on this. Trust him to make strong decisions for your and your family.

**20. Be honest and respectful.** Be honest (even if he doesn't want to hear the truth), but pick and choose your words carefully, because once you say something, you can't take it back. Children learn disrespect, disobedience, dishonesty, and disregard from their mother's actions toward their father.

**21. Love him more than you love your children.** Sounds crazy, I know, but never put your children before your husband. There is a natural order: marriage begins with two people falling in love, then children come along to be nurtured and loved, but never more than your spouse. Put your spouse first, because your children need to know how a marriage works and observing your partnership will keep their respect in place. Furthermore, when you and your partner remain in love, it provides stability for your children, no matter their age.

**22. Stand by him when he disciplines your children.** Never baby your children after he has punished them, at least until they have made up with their father. Uphold his rules and leadership in the family. Never disagree with him in front of the children and always present yourselves as a united front. If you disagree with him, express your thoughts to him privately.

**23. Lean on him.** Need him. Have him listen to you. Let him be your Superman.

**24. Never make him sorry that he came home to you.** Be his girlfriend. Men seek comfort in women, so make sure he comes home a clean house, a hot meal, soft, kind words, and back rubs. Always make him feel wanted.

**25. Keep what goes on in your house in your house.** Keep family and friends out of your business. If you are having issues with your husband, speak to him about it. When you add other people's opinions to the equation, the problems get worse.

**26. If you are mad at your husband, don't tell your family and friends.** You will forgive him long before other people who love you will.

**27. Don't expect your mother to take your side just because you're her daughter.** I'm sure your mother loves you very, very much. But if you are wrong, you are wrong. As long as your husband is leading, protecting, and providing for you, your mother should never help you badmouth him. She should send you back home to work it out. Remember that he must always be your head and you his heart.

**28. Your husband will act the way you treat him.** If you want a good husband, treat him like one. He will give you all that he has to offer. Treat him like shit and that's exactly what you will get in return.

**29. Don't nag.** You aren't his mother. Don't make demands of what he should or shouldn't do—he's a grown man. You can offer suggestions, but leave the final decision up to him.

**30. Make home his castle.** Treat him like the king that he is. A man should never rather be in the streets than home. His home should be a place of refuge for him, not a war zone.

**31. Ditch the granny panties!** Men are visual. Wear something sexy for him. Make him want you, not his momma.

**32. Keep God First.** The scriptural order of priorities is God, spouse, children, parents, extended family, and then the rest of the world. Keep God first in your marriage and everything else will fall in line.

**33. Never use sex as a weapon.** Women who use sex as a life negotiator will lose every time. So he made you mad or forgot to take out the trash. That doesn't give you the right to make him sleep on the couch. It's also a good way to ensure he will cheat on your ass. Men aren't made like women. They can't go without it.

# Chapter 17:
# I'm Not Your Friend,
# I'm Your Mom

If you're like me, you will want to be the cool mom. I like hanging out with my daughter and we have a good time together. However, there have been times when I needed to be her mother, even though she was still in "my mama is my friend" mode. Numerous times, I've found myself in a position where I felt disrespected, because she was talking to me any kind of way. A few times, I had to have conversations with myself: Who does she think she is talking to? Doesn't she know I will put my foot in her ass?

But she wasn't scared of me. She didn't think she was doing anything wrong and felt entitled to do and say what she wanted. Then, I realized that her attitude was my fault; I created that monster. I remember an incident or altercation that she and I had when she was a senior in high school. Her curfew was midnight. I called her to make sure she was okay and asked if she was going to have any issues making her curfew. She assured me that she was fine and would be home on time.

I trusted her. I fell asleep and woke up at 12:15, to find that she wasn't home.

I called her phone and it went straight to voicemail. I was about to lose it. Around one o'clock in the morning, she called, wanting a ride from the metro station. Well, I was determined to teach her a lesson—I refused to pick her up. I told her to walk home. After all, the metro station was just up the hill. But then, my husband offered to go get her, which made me angry, so I decided to just pick her up.

As I pulled up at the station, I saw that she was boiling mad. Why was she angry? I was the one who had to get out of my bed, because she missed curfew. She then got into the car with an attitude and did not say hi, dog, cat, thank you….*anything!* I was on fire. I stopped the car and asked her if she had anything to say. Her answer was "No!" That did it: how dare she have an attitude when she missed curfew? She was wrong, not me. We went back and forth for minutes before I told her to get out of my car. After she told me that she wasn't going anywhere, I faded to black and slapped the shit out of her. I thought it was over, but no: she hit me back. We sat there at the traffic light and had a hitting and shoving match.

Finally, I said "Okay, you don't have to get out, but when we get out of this car, I'm fucking you up!" That didn't stop her from mouthing off. We arrived at home and the next thing I knew, I was on her like white on rice. How dare she disrespect me? Who did she think she was? After things settled down, I knew exactly who she thought she was: she thought she was my friend and could treat me as such, and that was my fault.

One day you will be a mother, which is hard enough. But when you blur the lines between mother and friendship, you are bound to be disrespected. It's okay to be friends, but set limits. Know that there are boundaries that shouldn't be crossed and that when you cross them, there will be consequences. After all, you will be the mother, not the child.

**1. Don't lose yourself.** You don't have to give up doing the things you love once you become a mom. Find a way to incorporate those activities into your schedule. Yeah, I know: it's easier said than done. You may not be able to do things that you love as often as you did prior to having children but at least make an effort. You will be a happier mom if you find time to take care of your own needs. Happy mom = happy children.

**2. Don't be a Drill Sergeant.** Your kids aren't in the army. Yes, they need discipline, but they are kids. They are going to be messy, immature, and selfish. Find ways to teach those things they need to survive and succeed in life without being overbearing.

**3. Don't be an enabler.** Let your children figure things out on their own. It's not what you do for your kids that will make them exceptional human beings; it's what they are willing to achieve on their own.

**4. Don't be too much of a perfectionist.** Life is unpredictable and full of surprises. Being a control freak will only complicate things. You will make your life easier if you accept the fact that, sometimes, your house will be messy or that you're not always going to feel like cooking dinner. That's okay. Figure out what works best for you and your family and go with it. You make the rules, so it's fine to change them or even break them if it's going to make your lives easier.

**5. Screw the guilt.** Guilt is an absolute waste of time and energy, yet it is widespread amongst mothers. You aren't perfect. Being a mother will be new to you and you're going to make mistakes, saying and doing the wrong things on a regular basis. You won't be alone. There's an entire sisterhood of mothers that screw up—embrace it. Learn from your mistakes and move on. As long as you love your kids and provide a stable environment for them, they will turn out just fine.

**6. Have a lot of patience.** Raising kids is a difficult job. Kids are demanding, messy, noisy attention whores. Your patience will be tested on a regular basis. Take a deep breath, count down from ten, sit in your car and scream, or squeeze in a workout. Do whatever is going to help lower your blood pressure.

**7. Learn to listen to your children.** At times, we think that we know more than our kids, so it's difficult to listen to them. But take time to hear what they have to say. Sometimes they just need a listening ear.

**8. It's okay to be stern**. Set limits as far as what is acceptable and what is not. Your kids need a mother. By all means, listen to them, let them vent, respect them—but you are not their equal.

**9. Teach them simplicity**. You will do your children a big favor if you teach them early not to associate material things with happiness. Teach them the difference between needs and wants. Instead of buying books, borrow books from the library. Teach them to reuse what they can. Help them live a happy, simple life.

**10. Don't push them too hard**. As a mother, you are going to want your child to be successful, but don't push your kids to be overachievers. Rather, teach your children to reach their full potential. If you know that Johnny is not a great reader, don't push him to receive an A in reading. Encourage him to do the best that he can and help him set goals to get better grades.

**11. Teach them self-esteem**. High self-esteem is the single most important gift that a mother can give her kids. High self-esteem leads to self-respect values and will help your child live a more happy life at his or her full potential. They should always feel as if they can accomplish anything.

**12. Teach them to be self-reliant.** Don't rob your kids out of the opportunity to do things for themselves. If you do every chore for your children, you are not really helping them—you're crippling them. Encourage independence. Good parents work themselves out of the equation. As much as moms like to feel needed, it is important to let kids be as self-sufficient as possible.

**13. Have fun with your kids.** When you become a mom, it will be easy to get sucked into the day-to-day tasks of caring for your kids and then forget to enjoy their company. Kids are silly, so have fun with them. Create long-lasting memories. Get dirty. Throw on some music and dance. Play in the rain. Throw rules out of the window every now and then and just have fun. Don't worry, you'll have plenty of time to do the "Mom Stuff" too.

**14. Give your kids choices.** It will help them grow up to be liberated, decisive individuals, who won't settle for just anything. They will know exactly what they want and not be afraid to ask for it.

**15. Let your kids be who they are.** Always encourage your children to be the best that they can be. Never compare them to anyone else. They are who they are which should make them enough.

**16. Live in the moment.** Stop worrying in advance.

**17. Follow your gut instinct.** Always. If something doesn't feel right, it probably isn't. Find out what's going on. It's always better to be safe than sorry.

**18. You're not June Cleaver.** It's better to have emotionally healthy kids than a spotless house.

**19. Instructions are not available.** Kids don't come with manuals, so you're going to have to wing it.

**20. Show affection.** Hug and kiss your kids every day and tell them how much you love them. They should never have to wonder how you feel about them.

**21. You won't know it all.** Being a mom doesn't mean that you will know everything; it means you will be willing to be a student and a teacher at the same time, because every day challenges you with something new.

**22. Having a baby doesn't make you grown.** Don't get things misconstrued: just because you have a kid or two does not automatically mean that you are grown. Newsflash! If you are depending on other people to take care of you and your children (i.e. provide you with a place to stay, pay your bills, pay for daycare, etc.), you are not an adult. You're a child playing grown-up. An adult takes care of themselves and their responsibilities without any expectations from others. If someone is taking care of you and your children, be prepared for them to feel entitled to advise you on any and every thing. Don't like them apples? Then grow up, move out, and become the adult you want to be.

# Epilogue

Y ou're going to hate your mother most days. There will be moments where she won't be able to stand you either. Most daughters think that their mothers are squares who never did anything, don't know anything, can't tell them anything, and just don't get anything. That's perfectly fine: you don't need to know that your mother was a wild child who slept around, got bad grades, or was totally rebellious. All that is none of your business. As a matter of fact, it's best that she keep her skeletons in her closet (trust me, you don't want to know details of her past).

All that you need to know is that she is in your corner and that she loves you. There will be times when your mother will want to slap the shit out of you. Trust me, I've been there more times than I can count. But at the end of the day, it is important for you to know that you can depend on your mother no matter what. So, talk to her and have those tough conversations (even if they make you want throw up). Even though you can't stand her now, she will always be there for you. Whether you need a ride home because you drank too much at a party, need advice about sex, or just want a shoulder to cry on, she'll be there for you because she's your mom and you're her daughter…her baby girl.

In life there will be changes and challenges. I trust that this book will serve its purpose and save you a lot of heartache and pain from making the wrong decisions or having the wrong attitude about life. Don't go through life thinking that you have it all figured out. Trust me, you have a lot to learn about relationships, finances, and men. If I knew half of these things when I was younger, I would be a better woman, wife, and mother. I'm hoping that you will do as I say, not as I have done. Be the best you that you can be.

# About the Author

Dr. Tammy Jameson is a wife, mother of two, writer, and philanthropist. She earned her Bachelor of Arts in English at South Carolina State University, her Masters in Business Administration at the University of Phoenix, and her Doctor of Business Administration degree at Walden University. As someone who has experienced an abusive relationship first-hand, Jameson is an outspoken advocate for domestic violence victims. She volunteers her time and talents to numerous causes including ex-offender vocational training programs, domestic violence awareness, at-risk youth training programs, and serving as a consultant for small and disadvantaged organizations.

Jameson currently resides in Washington, DC, with her husband, Kevin, and son, Colin, and recently saw her daughter, Sejal (her inspiration for this book), off to college at Temple University. When she is not writing or volunteering, Jameson enjoys making arts and crafts, as well as repurposing furniture. She is a member of Delta Sigma Theta Sorority, Incorporated.

## WE WANT TO HEAR FROM YOU!!!

If this book has made a difference in your life Tammy would be delighted to hear about it.

**Leave a review on Amazon.com!**

---

**BOOK DR. TAMMY TO SPEAK AT YOUR NEXT EVENT!**

Send an email to: booking@publishyourgift.com

**FOLLOW DR. TAMMY ON SOCIAL MEDIA**

**f** DoAsISayNotAsIDo

---

"EMPOWERING YOU TO IMPACT GENERATIONS"

**WWW.PUBLISHYOURGIFT.COM**

CPSIA information can be obtained
at www.ICGtesting.com
Printed in the USA
LVHW052155180520
655844LV00004B/397

9 781942 838920